Rî.

Other Books by Graham Hartill:

Chroma
A Winged Head
Cennau's Bell
Ruan Ji's Island
Turas
Slipping the Leash (with Phil Maillard and Chris Torrance)
Tilt (with John Jones & Ric Hool)
Bronzes

Translations – with Wu Fusheng

The Seven Worthies of the Bamboo Grove
The Seven Masters of the Jian'an Era
Selected Poems of the Three Caos
Selected Poems of Cao Zhi
Songs of My Heart – selected poems of Ruan Ji

RHAPSODIES

Graham Hartill

For Amanda
" Thagne
a sparkling net !"

Grey
summer 2021

Aquifer

Published in the United Kingdom in 2021

by

Aquifer Books, www.glasfrynproject.org.uk

ISBN: 978-1-8383587-0-9

Cover image and other drawings: Tessa Waite
Cover Design: Aquifer

Contents

After Hokusai

(from the 100 Views of Pen y Fal)

Easter

(in appreciation of Albert Ayler)

Letters from America

Only Human

Crowd Scenes

Palaces

Migrating Bones

Life Stories

Lyrics

Notes

The Invocation of Kuya

After Hokusai

(from the 100 Views of Pen y Fal)

箱根國立公園
芦の湖の美觀

Romans View of Lake Side, Hakone

In these poems, our local axis mundi, Mynydd Pen y Fal, or Sugar Loaf, is figured as Fuji. They pay tribute to the great Japanese artist.

From the age of 7 or 8
I tried to write stories;
from 29 my poems were published here and there;
but until I was 70, nothing I wrote
was worthy of notice.

At 83 I was somewhat able
to fathom the growth
of plants and animals,
seas and people.

But, when I get to 110,
each syllable
will be squirming –
tadpoles in a net!

(after Hokusai)

for Ursula

Pink Light

the pink light
of the fine
work

a view: a cone
of rock
the other end of miles
of fields,
the hidden rivers,
a village

driving from town
on the back
roads

is yellow sky
around the mountain
or
there's grey

the mountain
holds
its infinite views
to itself

in yellow light,
in pink light
or

with the pinhole
of a star
above it

the fine work's
movement

Circumlocution

old quarrying:
harvesting
garlands of
rocks

the sparrows in
the art
   of green
high grass

a flat-winged raven
circling round
the jagged peak

is not
the soul of Basho

(too shiny)

*

Ta Hui said:
the last day
of your life
birth-and-death
come on you

the snake on my dark brown Japanese cane
crawls upwards

a monkey

grinning down at him
through half-closed eyes

Hot Summer Evening

love this rough and whitish road
with hardly any traffic on it,
rolling home at evening

*

Gynaecological tumour in old oak gables,
hot as it gets in the hedge-lane,
burst of mullein,
hawkweed

*

3-inch peacock flowers
    on a plum-branch,
squeak of buzzard, tattering heat,
    a window on fire

*

The names of the mountain:

peerless peak
    (fu ni: 'not 2')

    fire god
     (dreaming)

    the prosperous gentleman

    deathless

Proverbs of Sugar Loaf

If there's no room in your boots,
    put your feet in your hat

        (Spring)

Earth-mother:
a figure of speech

        (Spring)

Sugar-loaf,
sugar-daddy

        (Summer)

*"The moment of ceasing
is the moment the bird
enters the waterfall..."*

        (from a dream, Summer)

The oak in fog
like a big grey wing

        (Autumn)

"We've all pissed in the bath son...."

(on the Usk Bridge, Autumn)

The old fox
  has learned how to walk
on the cracking ice

(Winter)

"We all pat the bone"

(Winter)

thinking about the oldest songs –
    a white tambourine
  over Gelli Boeth

(Midwinter moon)

The sky dragged across like a heavy sack

(Winter)

The mountain does not work
for its clothes
or cook, boil water,

pick up coal for its stove:
   the mountain is a knife

   (Spring)

Crow vadis?

   (Spring)

"Bring me a bucket of sand
and I'll sing you the desert song!"

   (trad. Summer)

"Peace is the milk of birds"

   (from a Khartoum newspaper – Summer)

An inch above the path, a helicopter,
kicking up bee-dust

   (Summer)

Something's been nibbling
the Dark Sickener

   (Autumn)

A tree like a robe stitched with money

(Autumn)

The old burnt tree-stump lifted itself,
    then turned to face me

(Autumn)

A dragonfly wrapped in a cobweb

(Autumn)

My eyes keep missing the shooting stars!

(Winter)

fans and feathers of ice

Don't

       forget

the hill
that grew so slowly,
warming in your eye

the byre-tracks
  that come and go

the hare,

the beetle,

the crow's
    beakful of peel:

an orange flame
      in thin white grass

forget the day

    as bright as broken glass

Easter

in appreciation of Albert Ayler

A series in tribute to the American saxophonist (1936-70) whose unique, inspirational music draws on early, ecstatic sources for the great tradition: dirges, marches, gospel and folk tunes.

"Oh so smooth and easy did the music ease from the tenor's bell, with such tone, such feeling. When he began to improvise, this is when I became startled by the music's style. It was like the wind sometimes, moving fast, at other times it hovered, and at others it oscillated back and forth with sounds that would strike the earth to its centre, or soar until the penetration of the sky would clear the sky of clouds. He was speaking from or with his very soul, for himself and for me and for all the other people who wanted to discard certain values and judgments that had been deemed unalterable. As he played, Albert was a pilot of exploration. Upon recovery we told him how pleased we were with his exhibition..."

Errol Henderson

Smoke

Smoke from the riverbanks,
music, swelling into pleasure
borne downriver on the steamers,
deposited back into nooks
and elbows of thick Mississippi –

so soul
lives,
settlement persists –
it's the music,

the thoroughfare that is
the people's body
lilts
from entanglement of pain
into the wide time
of America's shout

and it is always Easter
whenever an artist discovers
gold
in the oldest songs
and redeems it,
shoving them onwards

to where they are ever wanted –
the white continents'
eyes consumptive, glazed
by capitalism,
banal,
and gagging for red soul-flowers

Easter Sunday morning –
listening out for
the giant Golden Day
of a trumpet bell,

the whipped ensemble of drum-skins,

the bowed bass

and the smoke

Flowers

The south is a bubbling heart,
the ten thousand things
full-grown, the chestnut
branches hooking towards the ground
its leaves big, wide open
hands, the thoroughfares of the lung,
its passages squeezing grain and water,
the Spirit's house
laden with happiness

mind
scorched, the body's flavour
bitter and excited,
the lips a
flying gate, from which
his songs,
the young and strong, to
fix exuberant blood

*

Woke up, her eyes were filled
with light
through a crack in the curtains,
bright yellow Sun
from nowhere,
winter ripped up

she strode through the room
a fissure of pure yellow energy,

balloon
of peace,
the smile on her head

with just the day in front,

its red
creative flower

The Bead

The blue Egyptian bead
turned up to be a folk-tune,
the fog drifting over the brown
ploughed field's wet shine
from Saturn via New York City;
it rustled on Malcolm X's wrist
stalking the terraced streets of Smethwick,
had lain in the world for generation
on generation, like a body, one
small outcrop of the future,
a comma of the total statement.

At the night's horizon,
the horn spins shining discs in the mind
of silver and lilac, increasing matter
in motor, auditory and visuospatial cortex;
corpus collosum, the bridge across the spheres,
beefed up.

Of violence and calm
a delicate balance:
the genius picks up his horn
and rams it into his TV screen in the Blank Hotel,
the house of his mind was putting up its last resistance.

Did the CIA kill Albert Ayler? Rephrase this:
the corporations ARE the terror of the Life-in-Death
of Houses, the gobbling, the babbling of power;
corpses set to banquet at behest of usura.

Faience is blue holy water, blue holy
river in the eye, blue beads,
a snake-like beauty in the living
changes of syntax.

*

Love reaches and unfolds,
a completed life
can show this:
                    Ayler,
dead in the water at age 34 –
his universe swims in the cup of his tune
forever: folk-songs are flowers, flowers
explosions of language – there is and there is no
silence in inner space, the thud of the blood,
the puling of nerves,
the picking up, between finger and finger,
of intimate stars.

            The tree in the ear,

            the Easter in the throat.

The Instruments

Memphis, Timbuctu,
turn up in an English field
their gates the song
in the soil
mouth
of our,
our,
wide green lyric

sand water ash
sets fire,
fire with copper
reforms the Gate of Bone
into blue little day
of the bead

and the heavy human skull
into bright green drum,
the vultures's wing-bone into
sonic
niche-culture ripeness

swollen through Ethiopia's gate
the horn of cultures
out to intense modern cold
we were
white, pink
brown, gold

making music
flit fingertips
punctures in stick of wing-bone
bright blue lyric,
red lyric,
forty millennia
cluttering
oestre gold

we broke through the upper Danube
into such condition,
20,000 years
of raven's breath made visible
collapsing onto earth,
down south
a bee in the mouth,
first music

*

vibrato yellow dawn above the river
freighted with cotton, hides,
primrose shoots up purple and lemon
the sun's up
elk bugle
cotoneaster fire
thorn berry
bloodred from icefields
white as a whistle

1967, Ayler playing
Universal Indians, the bitter cup

of a mountain of buffalo skulls,
laments for the smashed migrations
having fashioned
the hope of the trumpet bell
for sick brother Don
that tottered like dawn
emancipating at least
his lips

Art not being a measure for outlasting life
but a negotiation with ice,
the ghosts of love, he insists, dwell
in the bowed bass
and the bang catastrophe
of Sunny Murray's
dustbin tamtam,
whining register
of starving
spirit

the yellow gods of lily
swell through the thick heart
of the century's mud, being
funeral flowers, tough
decaying shadows
of these States

Love doesn't divide itself,
when the wood is gone
the wick burnt up,
the music occurs
in the thick bulb's need
and *only in praise's open space*
can grief take place, wrote Rilke
or: *"we stand on the edge of Hell,*

in Harlem, and wonder what we will do
in the face of all that we remember" –
Langston Hughes,
pinned up in Archie Shepp's apartment

New York's East River
with its cargo of humidity
flows always into its life
like music –
is there any other way to write
than to make it up as
we go along?
words come alive in the mouth

*

I'm sitting here
the blood-dropped cotton Easter
soon to burst with bees

the City on the Hill a ghost town
stars shine out
against the winter of the real

we happy *Paint the water, Write in dust*
capitalize whatever lives with gods
Breathe into Clay, to Play,
Hear, Vibrate
the Bright
Bell

Breathe
in Mother

Embouchure

Spring

Love Theory

all jewelry to his song

shots

at what Love requires

to try to be human

to wear the observancies'

necklace

upright through

the African bonegate

into the torturous west

a birdbone flute

concealed about his person

Water Music

If a man's root
is cut
his stalks and leaves will wither;
the detriment of the sinews is
they are unable to so contract,
take hold

the 5th detriment
is that of the bones;
a man cannot rise

      in winter the pulse is stone-like,
the ten thousand things are stored,
the East River laps at the city,
cold and brown and deaf;

its naiads whine for him,
his face in the back of a yellow cab
between two women, highballed, pink
– I see it – his little white beard
is smeared with Vaseline –
a smashed TV left back in the Blank Hotel,
his horn is the shining rain

That Afternoon

That afternoon
  his head is thickening

thick as this tarmac
  thick as this river

Give him some new temperature!

his head is as dense as a river

      Give him cool air,

  velocity,

   some rain

  His head

  is as dense as a well

give him a rainstorm

     and some cool air

Yelps from the quarry:

    the bones of the old countries

    splinter and crack

Give him a rainstorm

and clean air to follow

O
    give him some rain

        to wash out the river!

Give him some temperature

bright on his skin

Give him velocity,

rain,

    some compass

Give him some words from across the border

Give him some new

    grass

  to clean the river

    Give him some blue rain

Letters from America

What thoughts I have of you tonight, Walt Whitman! For I walked
down the sidestreets under the trees looking at the full moon.
In my hungry fatigue, and shopping for images, I went into the neon
fruit supermarket.
I saw you, Walt Whitman.
Where are we going? The doors close in an hour....

from Allen Ginsberg: 'A Supermarket in California'

Pay Dirt

*(Not just to make poverty history
but also excessive wealth!)*

Pay-dirt:
the metal of our work
that must be beaten, done –
in Colorado, Wales or Africa –
a long thin poem of the possible
for all the men and women who rolled across the blue, salt-ridden,
American grass,
mountain to murderous mountain –

Pay-dirt,
the mother-lode –

The last-time I was here, we were all being bombed by the television:
3 good reasons why Mohammed was a paedophile!
inevitability strafing the public mind
so when they actually invaded, it came as a mental relief,
some fact, at least.

*Fascism is inevitable in America, I've seen it all before:
they're spoiled, they're self-important, they don't know nothing,*
says Rafael, Auschwitz survivor.
*One more hit like that and the whole damn house of cards will collapse.
Cultural fascism?
Sure, why not!*

Outside places like this, - that's Boulder Colorado, or
Northampton Mass, or Berkeley,

say – *NO-ONE IS THINKING!*

and the president has demanded the contact details of everyone
doing research on
climate change.

Just like Germany before the war, I've seen it:
spoiled, self-righteous, ignorant:
Feel-Good movies everywhere!

Pierre Calonne, who fought with the French Resistance says:
I may be dying, but I'm dying with a snarl!
Listen: I know this man, in Arizona, he's a water lawyer,
a fucking WATER LAWYER! He knows about nothing,
nothing but water.
Another man I know knows all about screws
but knows fucking nothing at all about NAILS!
And then he retires and spends every morning
playing GOLF, then drinks and snores on the couch all afternoon.
His wife is smiling; out with his money, shopping.
My wife was close to the movie industry;
a man, a movie-mogul once said:
Never underestimate the stupidity of the American people!
Look, forget democracy,
your bank account knows nothing about it.
IT WAS A COUP d'ETAT!: I'm talking about George Bush,
it was a COUP d'ETAT, no doubt.

Rafael: *America? Look: The dog is barking, but the caravan just*
rolls on by.

Living in America, years have passed me by –
and I don't know anything about them!
Not just the odd weekend, but YEARS.

$5000 a month,
a goddam month,
to have my wife looked after.

Heard this one? An American man and a woman arrive in heaven.
It's white everywhere, of course,
with angels standing around,
and the woman is taking photographs and smiling,
and the husband is standing there with the suitcases.
"Smile everyone!" says the woman.
"My husband and I are just here for the winter!"

It was a coup d'etat.
Outside the enclaves, no-one is thinking.
When people die like this,
even death is astonished.
Curling blades of whipping steel
through Afghani air;
blood all over an ordinary morning's wind.

For Rafael, the fault is that of the entire English-speaking world;
the problem's that of the LANGUAGE community,
everybody else's enemy,
the language of enmity.
Poetry must grasp this;
poetry is the questioning of poetry.
Culture – in the face of it all –
why not?

Graham, you know the French say: "L'argent n'a pas d'odeur –
Money Has No Smell!"
Look, there's a couple of cowboys sitting on the crapper, a double-
holer!
One is pulling down his pants and he drops a nickel down the hole,
right into the shit!
He is disgusted.
Then his friend looks down the hole and drops a $5 bill –
imagine that!
A cowboy! How much does he earn a month?
A $5 bill! He drops this $5 bill right down the hole right into the
shit.

And then he gets up off the crapper and sticks his hand right in,
 right into the shit!
His friend says,
"Hey! You must be crazy! What are you doin'? Your hands are covered
in shit!"
And the other guy says,
"What? You don't think I'd stick my hand in the shit for a lousy nickel,
do ya?"

+

Boulder, Colorado

Letter from America

Never ending *dukkha,*

suffering –

call it, at least, anxiety –

this poetry for no other sake than life,

Life only

*

Stuck on a bus through downtown traffic,

wherever you are is stuff being sold –

it's us being sold –

Great Madness

*

Love,

your hand's so simple,

all your life of laughter

and all the unlaughable things

I'm imagining with my fingers,

my mind

dipping up against

your mind

*

sprinkles of light in Tiffany's shop at the airport

and in the museum

a little net

preserved by the desert,

8000 years old

*

Leaves in the Wasatch

sparkling lemon and

deep red orange –

big broad Utah sunlight,

crumbling crests of the mountains,

streaming cars below

*

on and on

up through the passes

to the high Lake Solitude and Silver Lake –

back in my room I put my silver Buddha

in front of the big black TV screen

*

In the double-elephant

Birds of America 1860

life-size pictures of black vultures

wrapping the corpse of a deer:

the black wings

canopy it,

dead recently

two birds

folded

in as one

and one

close up

and gazing into the shine

of a dead black eye

companionable even

just before

it breaks consideration

 of what does or doesn't

move

*

(Shakespeare:

Let vultures vile seize on his lungs also!

'Where is the life that late I led?' say they:

Why, here it is; welcome these pleasant days!)

*

Wine as blood

or symbol of blood –

if they'd thought of it only as metaphor

I guess them pioneers would never have even made it here,

been so driven

*

if they hadn't believed the lie

they wouldn't have lived

or live

*

a high array of enormous bone

in the Natural History Museum –

a wall of skulls

like cars

*

I'm not too good at the moment dear

but mostly they don't say anything,

the panhandlers

that thicken Market St.

or Library Square

*

perhaps it's illegal for them to speak

unless they're spoken to

*

between the orderly streets

these denizens of dirt

with hundreds of crazy addictions

mental illnesses

and bags –

so much more *visible,* I'm told,

since the crash of 2007

*

much more lit up

by the clarified streets,

the sparkling beacons of our disbelief

Some of the Alcoholics of Salt Lake City

This is the first architectural thrill
I've had for a while:
when you push into it, off
the snowy street, you're
inside and outside; the inside wall
stretching up to glass,
and the elevators
streaming up and down.
And coming and going, the –
what is the best thing to call them?
the frequenters of public libraries
at eight in the morning.
What do they call them these days in America?
Do they still say winos? Bums?
Homeless is the common word,
which is what they most certainly are.
Gliding up in the expensive lift,
you could get drunk on the fumes from their mouths;
there's three of them, and one of you
at this time in the morning,
light snow still falling in April.
From this side of the glass,
I'm not even sure what
books has got to do with it.

3 Psalms For That Year

after Psalm 9

Maintain the right and the cause.

Rebuke the enemy,

judge the wicked.

Put out their name for ever.

May their destructions come to perpetual end.

They may have got rid of Old Delhi, the Summer Palace,
the Great Plains Buffalo,

but their own memorials shall also perish.

Let there be a refuge for the oppressed,

a refuge,

in time of trouble.

after Psalm 12

The good man ceases,

the faithful fail,

speaking vanity with their neighbours;

with a double heart they speak.

These are pure words, as silver,

seven times tried in a furnace of earth,

and purified.

For the deliverance of the poor,

do they now arise.

after Psalm 49

Listen:

your mouth speaks truth

and your heart knows understanding.

Open your heart to the word

and open your own dark saying upon the harp.

Only Human

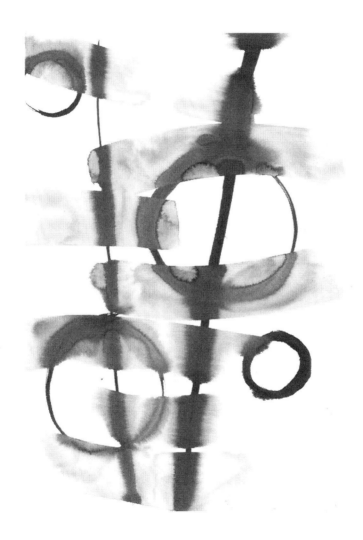

These poems are imaginary in that they are based on real stories and real men met during my work in prison but are composed from many sources.

My thanks to all the men and women I have worked with and contributed either directly or indirectly to these poems.

A Resolution

He wrote with the Devil's hand,
so he was strapped for writing.

Imagine the joy of forming a letter,
a G, on a page,
so slowly,
with your own left hand,
the curls in it;

imagine, years later,
having the time to do that here,
and nobody slapping your face for it.

When writing was the Devil's hand,
speech was the Devil's tongue –

if used against a priest that is.

He wanted to tell his dad,
but his dad was scared of his mother,
and his mother was nearly always drunk
and in hock to the priest,

who, passing by the fireplace,
would make a sign of the cross
ending with an eye-to-eye
and his finger softly
pressed to his lips:
It's our little secret…

Imagine being able now
to use that hand to form a letter,

then, making it through the tears,
to write the whole story you've never been able
to write

Lying

Your mum put out the washing by the railway line,
your dad was mad when he found you'd joined the army,
you were only 16 –
that I should be thinking about your stories
and all the other damaged stories on a day like this,
the sun on the snow
and the trees with the light on the snow on the branches –
birds lose 30% of their bodyweight
just sitting in their nests
on a night like last night, 6 or more below,
the roadway crusty and ridged,
the fields sharp white in starlight
with the big black wedge of the forestry
half a mile away –
that your story should all be bollocks –
I've got trouble with my memory –
Your dad was mad when he found you fiddled your age,
and then you were in Berlin
and there was a Russian car outside your flat at funny hours;
but nobody else believed you even about the army
and yes, my own belief was stretched
when all that stuff about secret ops came up –
but I believe you see in anything you think up,
I mean I believe in the thinking up of it,
I mean if you'd have called it *a* life story
instead of *your* life story that would have been okay
– would it – belief being somebody else's business?
Only in it for the stories am I?
But what am I helping you to do,
to lie better? Jimmy,
I heard what you did: the truth you tell yourself
let alone me, doesn't come into it –

your life is a jigsaw of damage and fantasy
the self you are left with is stuck here for good
and maybe that's the best for you, maybe you know that,
maybe that's the easiest for you, no scrabbling around
for the bills, and immune to your violent greed –
They said I was making it up
but I can't remember –
As long as you keep writing it, a kind of life appears,
a life in a book, a story of some life, some
life of kind, as long as you keep telling it,
as someone said, you're safe as a man behind a waterfall,
safe from the sound of any other voice –
that must be the effort anyway.
I bet you can't, Jimmy.
Your mum was hanging out the washing
your dad was down the steelworks.
The power station used to belch out
smuts of soot
like little black snowballs.

Imaginary

So I wonder where you are right now, Paul,
out there in the freezing morning I imagine,
north of Caernarfon; out there,
in the flat they got for you. I suppose
you should think yourself lucky:
at least you're out, out there,
and maybe you're in a small Welsh garage
blowing on coffee, obsessed with the wife and sons
that you're not allowed to see
maybe ever again,
your life killed off
by that obsession
about your father the priest,
your God the father,
your Virgin Mary daughter.

I don't know whether I can say this,
I don't know whether this poem is permissible
or whether you're likely to read it Paul and recognise yourself
or whether people will read it and recognise you;
I guess it's not unlikely
and therefore it's impossible –
but here it is.

(Now reader,
you could ask yourself if I've made Paul up.)

You were burning in your head,
your heart, which always did the right thing

so you thought, but never really did your *own* thing,
so you never became your own,
your old man writhing (I accidentally typed out *'writing'*!)
in your head.

     Is changing the name enough? What else is there
to change? Your real name can't go out into the world,
but what does it matter? There's lots like you,
but this isn't them.

     The thing with Christ,
I said, gesticulating upwards
to an imaginary space where the staircase is,
a tower of light blue metal and noise,
is that he takes on all our goodness,
leaving us with all the shit. I suppose
that's original sin. You were pained for a second,

  except that it wasn't you, as I've said, it was someone else.
It's no surprise we crave the pure image of a single man,
who's been stabbed and hung a million times, and lives:
out there in the terrible freedom;
                      is it too much
to expect just an actual life-story?

      No it wasn't Paul. Let's talk about Martin,
who'd lived his life beneath his mother's drunken mental weight
and her enslavement to the church, who told him when he was five he'd
killed his brother by measles, then found,
in the magic of writing it,
that he could be rid of that crushing fiction.

64

F's Poems

Did you have to say that?

While we were in the middle of this?

Let's just wish
there is a car around
for us to carry on –

we may come to some roads,
a car park,
with people in their cars –

let's see if they can help us.

I *would* be surprised.

If we do get from here,
it would be a good thing.

Did you have to say that *"Why?"*

*

I couldn't stick it at home
so I took a stroll
and when I got back that night
I was a bit the worse for wear

I went and took a long cool look
but the truth of it was
someone had just
exchanged my life for theirs

*

all my life is mine no more
that's the thing I never could tell
I hadn't thought it would be like this
and you never know
what happens to life that frightens us all

my life is on borrowed time

I leave it for you

Magnetism

My family?
look
imagine you had a handful of magnets right?
and you just tossed them across a table
how they fell –
some would be pulled together
and some pulled apart
depending

that's my family
how they landed

Only Human

Did you hear what happened this morning?
Somebody kicked off on A-block,
this lad.
This screw was spinning his cell
and he pissed him off,
he was pissed off anyway
because of the phones
and he pulled out a blade on him,
no, a homemade one.

No, this is what happened
that afternoon –
there was no-one else around
the central space,
the park between the blocks,
was empty,
everybody in industries
packing teabags,
silence.

I was heading between the blocks
– the blocks that are silver-grey,
steel-clad in the South Wales sunshine,
an estate of big silver fish-cans –
crossing to A-block, when out
of a door come these 3 guards
in yellow shirts, in a bundle,
between them with his wrist
crushed tight to his shoulder-blade,
a man, a young man, flopping black hair
and his neck bent back.
I didn't know Wyndham was actually that tall.

It was something I'd feared –
I knew he'd been pissed off
by being moved from wing, to wing, to wing –
What it is, he'd said as he slouched in the bending orange
                                        chair
in the B-block classroom stuffed with chairs
and several broken tables, What I want
is to write a poem to my girlfriend
but I don't know any good words
and Can you help me out?
I'm out in September. I
just want to write to her, Elaine,
she lives near Cannock – how I
just want to be with her and I can't
wait to see her and that.

No, this is what happened –
the screw had been fucking around on his phone-calls –
Hallo, this is Orange Telecom, it's costing you money –
and you only get so many calls in a month you see,
and then this screw was walking past his cell
and he just ran out and lamped him,
fucking lamped him! – Rog
was smiling, smiling at this,
as always – with a flask, 12 times,
and then the screws
were coming from everywhere man!
up the stairs, up the other stairs,
and Wyndham got his tele and he threw it at them see.

He's lost it now, his tele, and his parole, Gray,
anywhere else they'll have done him over,
fucked him up.

He can forget September now.

Entire

that the stone could be
   pulled from his chest
and become his father again

– that he could write an entire page
and his father be in it

Hermes

Hermes wanted to eat the meat
he'd killed for the gods.
His muscles were loose, and his mouth
water: he'd smelled the
beauty of burnt meat.

He stole a bone, some meat and fat
and hid it in his roof. It was a sign
he'd show his close associates,
and telling them he didn't give a fuck about the gods.
That'd be *his* story.

So men heard about this meat
and where he'd got it; they
were impressed, but
thought that he had to be mad,
and when it came down to it,
were scared.
No-body talked about it.

After all, *Only the very well-fed*
don't have to steal and lie,
and yet, they lie the most,
we'd mutter. *Good luck to him.*
Why should the glittering ones
get all the best hot juice
and fat? Why should only the virulent ones
own the rights of speech?

Hungry bellies are shameless;
the scent of roasting goat
is not too good for the likes of us.
We've also got places to go
things to be,
and stomachs to speak for us.

Crowd Scenes

We reach the idea of creation out of the experience of a face…. the order of creation is the order from which tyranny is excluded.

Emmanuel Levinas

Ken

400,000 languages

Ken, I dedicate this to you,
or to my memory of you –
you wouldn't understand it Ken
or would you?
Know what a poem can be?
Could you grasp this dedication?
No Ken, of course you can't,
because you're dead.
You sprinted across the Cowbridge Road
and got hit by a bus.
And your name was assumed.
I knew you, but you didn't know me,
you may have recognised me.
Everybody recognised you, who you were,
and your name was really Ken.
There's no need to protect you now,
it's been years, and anyway,
from what exactly? Why did I think
to call you Ron, or Jim? –
the bloke with the terrible stutter,
the learning disability.
Sometimes an enormous thing can flash
in the corner of your eye, too late.
Sometimes, from this side of the road at least,
something can look like an opening into the brain
where the world streams in, in a welter
that the world seems only one ingredient in.
No, I'm probably wrong, it's just what I heard –
you weren't killed running across the traffic
but yes, earlier, hit by a car,
because when I last saw you you were wearing callipers,
clumping up and down the fish and chip café on the

Cowbridge Road –
you fell and scraped your leg across the lino
and dragged yourself up, shouting *It's alright, alright!*
And you were always running all over the street, with your
shoulder down and sideways,
cleaving the breeze.
You said you'd run not 2, not 3 but
50 miles that morning,
to Newport and back,
yes 50 miles to Newport and back.
Muss ich einen
Zuschlag bezahlen?
Einfach hin und zuruck.
Es gibt einen zug nach Bonn
um neunzehn Uhr,
dort druken am Bahnsteig einz.
The astonishing thing is he could speak 10 languages –
we'd quizzed him in the caravan at work:
So give us Russian, Ken! –
Of course there were smiles,
and rolling eyeballs, but
Lo giorno se n'andava, e l'aere bruno
toglieva li animai che sono in terra
dalle fatiche loro; e io sol uno
m'apparecchiava a sostener la guerra
si del cammino e si della pietate,
che ritrarra la mente che non erra.
Italian then, Italian!
Italian, yeh.
He'd learned it all from Teach Yourself.
30 or thereabouts, his glasses lopsided,
I'd say Hello Ken!
and he wouldn't have a clue.
Or How's it going?
TO MARS AND BACK!
Somebody said they'd seen him stop on one of his sprints
to test his muscles,
lifted a car by its bumper, then carry on running,

76

through carbon monoxide
in 400,000 languages, muttering,
400,000 LANGUAGES YEH!
400,000 LANGUAGES! –
TO MARS AND BACK –

St Anthony's Well

in the Forest of Dean

Jane gets up to read her poems barefoot;
looking less crumpled tonight,
in good possession.
How many grandchildren?

> *I'm trying to cope with my drinking. My life's a mess*
> *and everybody else's who comes into contact with me –*

One who suffers a fire;
St Anthony, herdsman,
cool her history.

*

There are different kinds of drop out –
those with proper jobs, who like to dress up and express themselves,
and those who face or suffer St Anthony's mental fire
every day:

Special Brew swilling, deep in the Forest of Dean,
their faces hot in the firelight,
volleys of gunshot laughter,
rutted red tracks between the trees;

the women who hustle the day
from shop to relatives' houses in terraced valleys –

even they make poems, they get it together,
barefoot, stepping lightly,

get up on their throbbing nerves
& love it afterwards.

Jane! Your getting up there at all
is an idiom,
even an ideology.

After the Workshop

Hundreds of times it is by now
I've seen the way people get
lit up,
their bright words occurring together,

when the problems of being together,
of speech, are put aside,
and we salvage our right to beauty.

See that guy in Luigi's after the workshop,
he has no brotherhood, his
face is dull, but he knows what he wants,
it is haddock and lager.

Friday, he might have enjoyed our theme
of *Poetry and Winter* –
Joan had said she loved her food
and presented, laughing, in front of us,
her poem of chicken and pies

and Andrew said that the light of Winter hurt him
but he was better when the little sun went down

and Simon said he'd send us his greetings;
God knows what his life is.

Men in the café, you know what you're missing –
the world is very rich.

The man with the thick black coat and the yellow drink
is in love.

Palaces

Men fashion unfreedom as a bribe for self perpetuation....There is no other way to speak. What began in religion remains religious. All power is sacred power, because it begins in the hunger for immortality; and it ends in the absolute subjection to people and things which represent immortality power.

Ernest Becker

Pebbles

(St David's)

1

Heatwave, upset
to the stomach,
forgetfulness: ordinary
stuff –

      but the TV News:
annihilation
   drifting
up through the floorboards:
     Gaza –

how can we grasp it
in the enforced amnesia, distraction
from what a simple little body is, a
    single child?

   If I could just meet history,
and shake his hand! If we could just behold
   an X-ray of the authentic body –

2

pickings
from beach or sky,
faces, up against

faces,
listenings –

       how else to meet the oldest stories
face-to-face, of selfhood,

let alone land-grab?
How else learn by our mistakes,
language, rubbing up against language,
little cultures
within the big Economics,
resisting it?

       What choice do we have
but to listen close,
with our own voice,
meeting being
the making of meeting?

       There used to be Bear along this coast,

   and Wild Boar –

3

Of course we don't really forget
the essentials, they transmute; we'll reap the
Gaza wind alright, we already are:
               501
of our children killed today,
and in the middle-eastern scheme of things
   it's a skirmish –

4

Sometimes it seems the prisoner of life
inherits his imprisonment
from the wrecked hearts of his parents,
succeeding from their own
savage, deprived light –

                    but Death,
like cathedral stone, isn't violent, just Culture:
the beautiful carving of bear or leaf
on the fortified tower, and yes, of course,
a poem –

                    in a Christian cross,
the violence done
to Love
can coalesce: this is maybe how
cultures solidify –

5

The body's limits
ache, withdrawing from the sun, a failing eye-muscle,
wandering round St David's cathedral territory:
fish-traps, engineered caves and
crumbling lintels –

                    amazing they can even
get the scaffolding balanced
up there on the roofs!

The sun on the headland, north,
an orange butterfly –

6

If one or two people
think something, people say it's autism,

if three or more, it's culture!

What is any body?
a tower in starlight,

any body
of work that is,
it's purplish rocks so perfectly dressed,
so knowing of itself –

                    you see,
my problem is, that working with the men I do
you tend to suspect everything, see every story
as what it is,
                    a version of events,
know that it's everything stories –

but still,
the tower
is beautiful, stretching
to starlight –

             without this body,
beauty is impossible, measure
impossible –

7

The little girl
plays with her family in the sand –
bashing sand, learning
what sand is, what it is
she is with sand –

                    I'm staggering
like a beetle on the dusty path
up the cliff; the
world's distinctions, I think,
are like peoples: the headland, the sea,
and even this path –

8

                    the mind is only alive
in contact with the thing,
including thought

                    that leans like a moth
against the lit-up wall –

                    things
like people talking,
X-ray of an accidental touch,
the gravity of eye-contact –

                              the earliest beauty
     that of the pebbled hand-axe:
     divinely superfluous –

     its gleam
     that of organismic
     thriving:

     the orange moth

     abundant here
     in sea grass,

     common –

From A Chained Library

(the ornaments of power)

1

Today I try to look into the face of things –
    the worlds request attention
  to suffer our honour –

play with lightness –
    a grin, the hitch of a shoulder,
  just come and go,
    and work demands only itself –
      the human lotus, swelling over crippled water,
        opening into time,

    which is the story of any life.

A life-story opens time,
    holds birth and death apart,
  stops time collapsing –

    bewilderments,

      this is, after all,
      the World.

    *

2

These bloody jets rend gashes in my concentration,
      ripping the hills –

     My son bends over, smothering his ears –
        "You could see the pilot's face!"
     They nearly took the lid off,
        then they're gone, to Pembrokeshire,
      tilting at the coast by now,
         a shuddered thrall of superheated gas:

     a ritual –
just like making cars is a ritual.
   like making guns,
     like making money. Money out of money –
   rituals of immortality,

     and art is also a time-machine,
       at Patricio, or Kempley,
       the altar of the human body –

3

In violence we act as if we were alone.

The jets that cleaver-hacked the sunny mountain sky this
                          morning
          are only ornaments of power –
       titanium jewels in a crown that will survive
             the death of only kings.

       Like children, we are keepers of the sacred texts,
               we want the same story, over and over again –
           a theocracy's job, or a capitalist's,
                          is to chain the text –

          but life is a language, a touch, and a timing:

             faces flow past,
                 the altars are way markers –

          and every lost book a lake
                 in which we are free to imagine.

                 *

Votive

Coracles, warships,
drifted into just below us,
surprisingly;
the Severn is way off nowadays,
wide and shining:
pylons, wires, warehouses –

we endure
an ever-shifting planet
and dreams
that we hopelessly try
to leave alone

stones of an architecture
stuck on the hill
to incubate visions:
little hands
with curled-in nails
show iron deficiency –
votive offerings

a 6-inch perfect greyhound,
bronze, looking over his shoulder –
the dream of a perfect body
is a thing this place is for,
of incubating a form
that works, the
interlocking of wildfowl,
reeds and salt

and fish: the economy
and the archetype; Richard
corrects me: the archetype cannot
be known, but it brings us
images

imagine a sparkling net:
if you agitate it in
one place, the net
shudders and rustles,
whispers –
  fish
are brought to light,
though fish, of course,
can never be known

*

Nodens, the god of this place,
is Núada, the fisher, the hunter, the
Catcher with the Silver Hand;
you can wear his bracelet,
come into contact
with his finger

your body being a net
perhaps, and the interstices
of your mind
where images
happen:
imagine the salmon-leaps
in Roman times

the fight against the current
of life, to get back,
back, to where you are strong
enough to win,
to earn your reproduction,
to where you can use
your dream

*

a poem
that makes the light

is still required, yet
the lurcher
snuffles in leaf-mould,
loving the fat rank world
where the dream lurks –

agh!
that's where we are from

*

this to the God, to the Dream:
please allow the paradox
of healing,
while getting old!
please incubate Love,

the good art
being that
which allows the unfolding
of images,

dreams
being action
of all the glorious Other

*

Migrating Bones

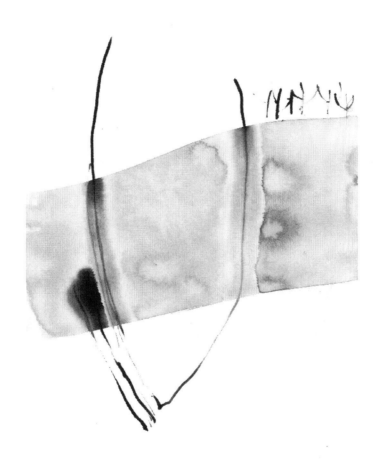

dedicated to Anne Cluysenaar

1936-2014

"in search of a world"

Migrating Bones

1

Kilmartin

Sunshine and showers'
brilliance
veering up the valley

writing food for the hungry ghosts,
a single tooth
in a cairn

a child's tooth,
6 or 7,
the rest of the bodies
gone
by acidic vapour

but pieces of polished jet
from an important necklace

and a little girl's,
or little boy's tooth
in a grave-cist

with its bafflements,
false entrances –
even ghosts can be fooled it seems,

spirit
being more of what we don't know
than of what we do

*

In a shiny green notebook from San Francisco
embroidered with dragonflies

new worlds
and old
to the page –

Hokusai, Ornette Coleman,
rustling in the mind

the poem's
tribute,
response

the lochs aglint
through our roaming windscreen

feeding Hovis
to ghosts
and water-birds

*

The people who lived in Kilmartin
were us,
new settled
with realization:
we stand
on our own two feet

and grown to the moment of speech,
self-consciousness,
loss:

the tooth in the grave-cist –

animals can only grow more fur,
but man moves things around –

this is a field we lead each other to
for thousands of years, making the story of self
from scatterings of reflexion –
all we have to go on, work with,

slowly knowing
cause and effects
that now we speak of happiness, good attachment
being vital, good attachment
being freedom, erecting
a circle of stone in Argyll

*

                    Love
we found,
isn't easy to bring into being,
it comes with fear,
is held
when landscape is ceremony,
the ceremony
of growing up,
of making circles
and paths
and finding
a next
moment

erecting this theatre, poem,
this ceremony of art,
this life for the dead
in the heart's field

*

In Denmark, 6,000 years ago
a woman and child
were placed in a grave,
the child laid down
on a swan's wing

nearby, a man
with a set of antlers –

moonset
at 60,
        take little for granted,
a tooth in a cist
left over by nature's acid

the redshank's
pilililiu
        the flight of the invisible –
knowing writing itself
is a metaphor

a polished ammonite spiral,
a jewel, a solid thing
where inner and outer movement
are the same

grown into
this sentence,

an arrowhead,
keen,
of lilac stone
amid dangerous stars

laid down
in a swan's wing

2

Migrating Bones

But aren't they always?

and isn't this
the oldest thing
of all

the dead being wild,
being out of control?

the spirits,
bones,
heading back to the woods?

that forestry beyond the ridge,
Coed Ddu,
before they felled it –

one winter day I wouldn't go in,
so dark
and thick with snow –

a vast heavy roof
and the thinnest light
in the avenues

or that dream, in the early 80's,
of ashes
whispering down the chimney –

only that –

I woke afraid –

went the long way round instead
trudging through fields of dazzling snow

*

Edward Thomas left a feather
of presence,
a signal
for anyone to follow

yet, if we do follow
must it be all the way

to the suicide of war
(war being suicide by other means)
not just into one's unconscious
but the *world's* unconscious,
an *unfathomable*
depression?

that won't do, of course –
even calling it such,
just calling it,
reels it in
and makes it comprehensible,
manageable,
language bringing the open world
into being,
meaning
negotiation
with open light

and any agreement dependent on us
using of course
the same currency:
Trust –

not just the unconscious
but an unconscious beyond the unconscious,
the *wild*,
the fangs!
the eyes of the dog in chase
its major joy,
the exuberance of its life

being what terror is for –
it's fight or flight

and my own terrors?
drowning,
the fear of being out of reach
of my own interior mother

half-way through Dante's Wood,
or call it
Wilfred Owen's profound dull tunnel,
Eliot's London Bridge,
Hansel and Gretel's European forest

or that prisoner's story that haunts me
of looking out from Chiron's boat at all the houses
we have built in life
in tumbling ruins
(shall we say like Babel?) –

all you have made in life
pulled down –
it is war,
the ruins of deserted cities,
the post-industrial coming to nothing
I grew up with,
out of

and it is finally
the mystery
of our bodies,

the brain
the darkest and most complex forest –

so what shall
I leave then?

a new feather?

(Edward Thomas: The Green Roads
Anne Cluysenaar: Shetland Ewe)

3

Pearl

The pearl, the uncatchable girl,
refuses resurrection:
she needs to say put –

Eurydice,

Pearl

of course we look back,
because it is written,
a Law –

and she must stay
to be changed
in the flow of death

there is grieving
and ritual,
the need to home the bones –

the burial chamber
comes with being settled,
with civilisation

when dog-eats-dog,
especially the bones,
has been tempered,

the landscape somewhat
softened

now we can, in part, control
the settlement,
keep the wolves out,
by which I mean
other men

we 'preserve ourselves' –
in the face of what?
of God
come alive,
with the need to know Death

and Love
come alive
of great price

Life Stories

My Dad In His Suit And My Mom In Her Dress

You look beautiful
you two
when you are young

with your hair and your clothes
that you afforded

Mom says she knocked that dress up before you went away

- such skill!

like Dad's with saw and glue

this is the simplest poem

you look beautiful in that photo

For Years

For years
he spent his days
2 weeks on
and 2 weeks off
on nights
putting doors on cars
the year on year
of *a living*
keeping up with the conveyor-belt
no good
if you had a skiver in your gang
and bonuses lost –
"get rid of him"

night on night
she'd be up late
a bit of peace and quiet in the kitchen
ironing shirts like they'd never been out of the packet
sewing on buttons
reversing collars
mending like you'd never know

growing up like any kid
oblivious to their lives
to what they did off-stage
that's how they made a life
for us
I'm fierce for that –

that's why I'm building them
this clutch of time

Glamour

(in an old blue handbag)

The powder

and the letters

and

the old photos:

the brothers in military caps

are handsome

as handsome was;

the newer photos:

families on beaches

next to 1960's cars,

in colour, when colours were rare.

She came from a world

when nothing was surplus, of

want

and dread of want:

you worked for it,

you worked

for the powder,

the little car,

the carpet;

you worked for

the blue leather handbag,

the purple see-through sweet wrappers,

the hearing aid batteries,

you worked for the

marriage,

you fought

for love of colour

Lyrics

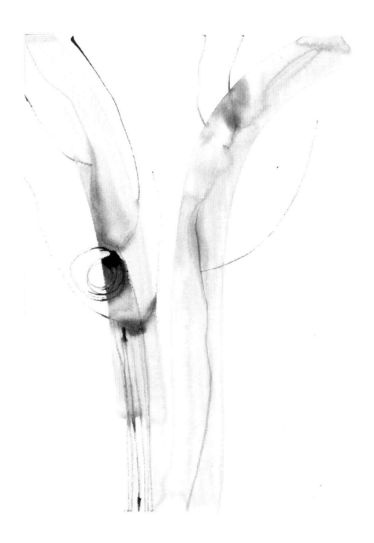

From Silbury Hill

'For I am the fastest mama / flash
   of creamy light
      between the rain

    *

          the adder flies
        to my ankle,

         my mattress is swollen
        with corn and cattle

    *

I swell from populations
   past and passing

    *

         an acrobat,
        I vault the middle of Nature
        – increasing dancer'

Now

We have overcome all enemies but ourselves

*

(the twin-staffed man on the font
   and serpents in stone
at Avebury:)

His friend the ground,
   his self
stood up between his double rods
   held upright in his outstretched hands

     measures the width of the stars' rotation,

the stretch of the snake at his feet

*

a man is his tribe
   and our living
the flow of the stream

a grass-snake's curl through fields,
its flourish, the hope of
a kill in the woods

his enemy being his stomach:

an unseen wolf
between sharp stars

The Value Of Wild And Tame

The lineage of bees is all the way from Paradise,
the mass cannot be sung without their wax
    – three free huntings for a swarming branch.

The fox and otter, since they have no habitation
and are always on the move,
and for the badger,
    we can set no legal value.

We have kids and are looking for brighter fields
and greener money,
yet intensive farming's rubric's
slithery as spraint:
they say –
    it's for him who <u>buys</u> to look for outward harm…

The weather-pole,
the thatch-spar
and the fireback
cry out:
    Preserve the Woods!

The sweet and sour apple
hold their court

        (from the Laws of Hywel Dda)

Lyric

for New Year

May the complex of woods
thicken,
daffodils suddenly widen
the bend of the road

the new, the
old story
waiting for me, that's you,
to make it

a broken barn's
tatters, collapse
of a hundred years

blackthorn and birch
refigured
from ancient genes

and born, reborn,
the wren's fleet
shudder of vowels, a
billion apprehensions
of the river

New Year

2017

first ice-ponds on the side of Sugar Loaf:

Just
the earth

a fragile surface

800,000 years (?)
of not much more than arrowheads,
then we *decorated* them:
thus possibility,
culture –

human being

a fragile surface

*

the ground drifts round
beneath our life

a bright wind
in a blue sky

guidance:

feathers

balance an arrow-shaft

*

constancy:

and up the mountain:

holding the mind

in the mind's hand

Frost

bristles on metal,
thick leaves'
flesh

the sun on the hill
burns off
the mirror-ball

mirror-bright beauty,
and always
an anxious seed:

just how cold is the Winter really going to be this year?
Can we stay warm
on a planet getting warmer?

a matter of 1° or so:
nature's thought is as
delicate as frost

determines the sex
in the egg
and the safety of earth

delicacy – I like the word

the diamond
eye of December
winking

Spring

I'm telling myself some things that I already know:

that love always wrestles with loss,

that, being human, the fight is always between the real and the
how we would like it to be,

that, being human, pain is right where beauty is,

yet still we can speak sometimes:

a poem, being like your life,

you want it to be some good

*

the wind is suddenly loud in the bushes,
wrapped inside the hill
the cuckoo's
song

the birds on the road in the morning are hypnotised by sex-drive!

Spring is the time of the dangerous
jamming of brakes
for the sake of sparrows

The Exotic Earth

(food)

I'm thinking about the exotic earth:

flashing trees in

warm wind,

dawn on a southern beach

with poor huts,

a scarlet sun

and a cold sea:

the Scottish North Atlantic

hauling its fluid

creatures, billions

of different greens

and rainbow crusts of rock –

in China, I

remember,

wagon-loads of

cabbages,

in Massachusetts,

hills of pumpkins –

how we live by biting into

green

ginger,

swarming,

love like

juice

Love

*"after the searching they found all the parts of Osiris
except his phallus which had been swallowed by a fish"*

*

The buzzards will carry your body away to the tops of the
forest, Mynydd Du,
the Black Forest,
it will be harvested when the trees are,
it will be harvested into the sky

the fox will carry your meat away
to fill her pantry
because it is in her mind to do so

the spiders will carry your soul
to a million places

*

the oaks and birches along the Grwyne Fawr
remember what it is to fashion a place
beyond the reach of any phrase –

this giant silence

belongs to them

Notes

After Hokusai

The Chinese master Ta Hui Tsung Kao (1089-1163) is a central figure in the Rinzai tradition of Zen Buddhism.

The little 'proverbs' are owed to Chris Torrance for his sequence *Wet Pulp* (the sayings of the three miserable bards of the island of Britain) which I first read in the publication *The Slim Book / Wet Pulp,* published by Stone Lantern Press in 1986. It can now be found as Book 5 in Chris's *The Magic Door* published by Test Centre in 2017.

Some of these poems previously appeared in Scintilla.

Easter

The pianist Errol Henderson is quoted in: *As Serious As Your Life: Black Music and the Free Jazz Revolution* by Val Wilmer, published by Serpent's Tail, London.

Some of these poems were performed with Lyndon Davies as part of the Gelynion series of performance events in Swansea in May 2015.

There are references in the sequence to tracks from Ayler's recordings: in particular in 'Flowers' to two tracks on *'Love Cry'* (1968) and in 'Water Music' to the last track on *The Last Album* (1971).

The reference to the blue bead is from Peter Riley's influential poem, *Did the CIA Kill Albert Ayler?* which appeared in Poetry Review Vol 65, nos 2&3.

'a snake-like beauty in the living changes of syntax' is from Robert Duncan's *The Structure of Rime 1*, in *The Opening of the Field.*

'corpses set to banquet at behest of usura' is from the 45th Canto of Ezra Pound.
'The tree in the ear' is from Rilke's *Sonnets to Orpheus.* Thanks to David Cook for his translations, published by Redcliffe Press in 2012.

Many thanks to Ian McLachlan for his piece *The Coming of Albert Ayler*, published in Junction Box Issue 2 (see Glasfryn Project online).

Letters from America

The illustration is from a performance at the University of Massachusetts, Amherst in 1978, as is the picture on the back cover.

These poems were written during and following a series of trips to Salt Lake City.

The Shakespeare quotation accompanied the display of Audubon's Birds of America in the City Library. It is from *Henry IV Part One*.

The psalms are redacted versions from the Old Testament.

Only Human

Some of this work was published in Poetry Wales 53:1, Summer 2017.

For more on Hermes as the first liar, see *Trickster Makes this World*, by Lewis Hyde.

Pebbles

With many thanks to Sylvia and Mark Perry, in whose house "The Pebbles", in St David's, Pembrokeshire, the poem was written.

The quotation about culture & cults is from Sheldon Solomon, of the Ernest Becker Foundation. The earlier quotation is from Becker's book *Escape from Evil.*

From a Chained Library

This is in Hereford Cathedral.

Patricio and Kempley: two favourite churches, both noted for their medieval wall paintings.

Votive

was written after a visit to the Roman remains at Lydney, Gloucestershire with my friend Richard Lanham, to whom the poem is dedicated with thanks for a near-lifetime of explorations.

'We know that the temple was dedicated to an otherwise unknown god called Nodens, known as 'the Catcher', who had a magical hand. Nodens evolved in Irish legend as Nuada ('of the silver hand') and in Welsh folklore as Lludd Llaw Ereint, the inspiration for Shakespeare's King Lear.

Nodens may have been a god of fishing, but it is equally likely that he was a god of healing. Archaeologists discovered a huge number of votive offerings on the temple site, including quantities of bracelets, pins and models of dogs. In Roman religion, dogs were thought to aid in healing and were often used in Greek and Roman temples to lick the afflicted part of the body to speed healing. Archaeologists also found numbers of tablets inscribed with healing requests.'
from: https://www.britainexpress.com/attractions.htm?attraction=2502

Migrating Bones

Kilmartin Glen is in Argyll and holds a very significant concentration of Neolithic and Bronze Age remains.

Anne's poem *Shetland Ewe* can be found in her collection *Migrations* published by Cinnamon Press in 2011.

A version of section 2 of 'Migrating Bones' appeared in *At Time's Edge: remembering Anne Cluysenaar*, edited by Fiona Owen and published by the Vaughan Association in 2016.

My appreciation of Edward Thomas has been enhanced by Matthew Hollis's biography: *Now All Roads Lead to France: the last years of Edward Thomas*, published by Faber & Faber.

Pearl: the medieval poem and also Barry MacSweeney's intimate sequence in *Wolf Tongue: Selected Poems 1965-2000* published by Bloodaxe.

Love

'after the searching...' is from Jules Cashford's book, *The Myth of Isis and Osiris,* published by Barefoot Books.

The Invocation of Kuya.

Kuya, (903-972) 'the holy man of the market place', was an itinerant Japanese Buddhist monk who added music and dance to his prayers, and carried out works for the public benefit such as burning abandoned corpses, building roads and bridges and digging wells.

Many thanks to the anonymous photographers of Mt Fuji, Albert Ayler as a Boy, the greyhound and Kuya.

The Invocation of Kuya

(carved by Kosho, 13th C)

When you speak, the tree
happens; when you sing
the world begins to spin
in the bone-house; I
would believe it, *now*
being the urge of a voice, its
coming forth as flower, bird or rock,
or as Kuya: people wriggle from his lips
like sprats on a line, like saplings,
syllables of wood –
Kuya, wandered around, did good,
anointing corpses left on the edges
of woods and in ditches
with oil, and setting fire to them,
invoking 'immeasurable light'
in the body-mind, in the life-and-death
of the man, woman or child.
I would believe it: for Mack
whose words are a fever of dissociation,
God as speech defect; and Nick,
who wrote for me of hell: the houses
we've built in life, all tumbling over,
and over again, as we helplessly watch
from the boat of passing over –
Speaking, the world
spins round and round in the skull; sung to,
the baby is personified,
the song laid down in her mind
forever, safe and coming forth. We
hear it: the man or the woman is made
in the child: I am not a fish, nor a door,
nor syllable of wood.

137

The world is
like a cloud of starlings, the sentence
being Love. What's possible?
Love-songs, shouted out
like lilies.

Rhapsody means 'stitch song', a rhapsodist one who recited, stitched together and improvised on various elements of epic poetry. In a more general sense a rhapsody may be an emotional, perhaps even ecstatic, utterance.

from Cuddon's Dictionary of Literary Terms

The nameless was the beginning of heaven and earth; the named was the mother of the myriad creatures.

Hence always rid yourself of desires in order to observe its secrets; but always allow yourself to have desires in order to observe its manifestations.

These two are the same but diverge in name as they issue forth.

Tao Te Ching